The Li

by Christopher Stitt

illustrated by Luke Jurevicius

⊠Harcourt Achieve

Rigby • Saxon • Steck-Vaughn

www.HarcourtAchieve.com
1.800.531.5015

Characters

Benny

The creepy little man

Contents

Chapter **1**

Warning

Benny was tired. His feet were sore, and his stomach grumbled. Every hotel in town was full, except for the spooky-looking one at the top of the hill.

"There's only one room left. It's in the attic," said the creepy little man behind the hotel desk.

"I'll take it," Benny sighed.

The man held out the key and grinned. "Whatever you do, don't open the little box that sits on the table."

"All I want to do is eat and sleep," said Benny as he took the key. "I'm not interested in a little box."

The man laughed as Benny climbed the stairs. "Everyone who takes the room says that. They all end up running from the room in terror."

Benny was a bit worried by what the man said. But he had to get some sleep — he was so tired. All day he'd been trying to sell the new Zoom Vroom motorized broom. He hadn't even sold one.

Chapter 2

Inside the Room

Benny walked into the room in the attic. The window was boarded up. The bedside table was smashed.

The bed looked good, though — soft and warm.

Benny fell onto the bed and sighed.
"This feels great."

His stomach grumbled again. He sat up.
"I wonder if this hotel sells any food?"

That was when Benny saw it. A beam of moonlight lit up the little box. It was small and made of wood. "Don't be silly, Benny. You don't need to open it," he told himself.

The creepy little man made Benny a
toasted cheese sandwich. Benny ate it
in bed. He never took his eyes off
the box. Something inside him said,
"Open the box, Benny!"

Chapter 3

Open the Box!

Benny turned off the light and tried to sleep. He tossed and turned. All he could think about was the box. "Open it! Open it!"

Benny climbed out of bed. He put on his bathrobe. "Don't be silly, Benny. Nothing scary could fit inside such a little box!"

Benny lifted the lid slowly. A little green monster jumped out onto the table. Benny screamed, "Help!"

The monster gurgled and laughed.

Benny ran from the room. He looked over
his shoulder. The little green monster was
running down the stairs after him. Benny ran
past the front desk.

"I told you not to open it," said the creepy little man.

"Help!" shouted Benny as he ran into the night. He turned around. The little green monster was still chasing him.

Benny saw a bike in town. He jumped onto it and rode along the streets. His legs pumped. His head was wet with sweat. He looked over his shoulder. The little green monster was still chasing him.

Chapter 4

Tap, Tap, Tap

At the seaside, Benny jumped on a ferry. The bell dinged, and the ferry pulled away from the pier. Benny sighed, "Now I'm safe."

He looked over the railing. The little green monster was swimming after the ferry. "Oh, no!" gasped Benny.

Benny leaped from the ferry as it docked
at the city pier. He climbed into a taxi.
"Get me out of here, fast," he shouted at
the taxi driver.

The taxi driver sped along the road. Benny looked out the back window. The little green monster was running behind them.

"Take me to the train station," he told the taxi driver.

Benny jumped aboard an express train,
just as it was leaving the station. He
slumped into a seat, gasping, "He'll never
catch this train."

Benny peered out the window of the train. "You've got to be kidding!" The little green monster was racing along beside the tracks.

When the train came to a stop, Benny jumped out. He caught a bus. The bus drove through busy suburbs, around corners, and down one-way streets.

"There's no way he can catch me now," said
Benny to himself. "I've lost him for sure."
He closed his eyes to sleep.

The bus stopped at a red light. Benny woke with a jump. Something was tapping on the window next to him.

Chapter 5

Trapped

"NO!" shouted Benny. The little green monster was grinning at him. Benny jumped off the bus and ran down the street.

Benny turned a corner and came to a
sudden halt. "A dead end! I've run into
a dead end."

He turned around slowly.

The little green monster was still after him.

"I give up," Benny shouted. "I can't run anymore. I'm too tired." He closed his eyes and waited for the little green monster to eat him.

Benny felt a finger touch him on the leg.
"You're it," the little green monster
gurgled.

Glossary

attic
a room in the roof

express
a fast train

grumbled
complained

gurgled
made a bubbling sound

halt
stop

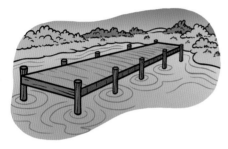

pier
something built in the
water for people to
walk on

suburbs
places where people
live near a city

terror
strong fear, panic

Christopher Stitt

The Little Box is a story I made up many years ago to tell at a Scout campfire. It changed a little bit every time I told it. The last group of children I told the story to enjoyed it so much they convinced me to write it down. I like this story because the ending is unexpected — fear turns to laughter when the little monster says, "You're it."

Luke Jurevicius and Toby Quarmby